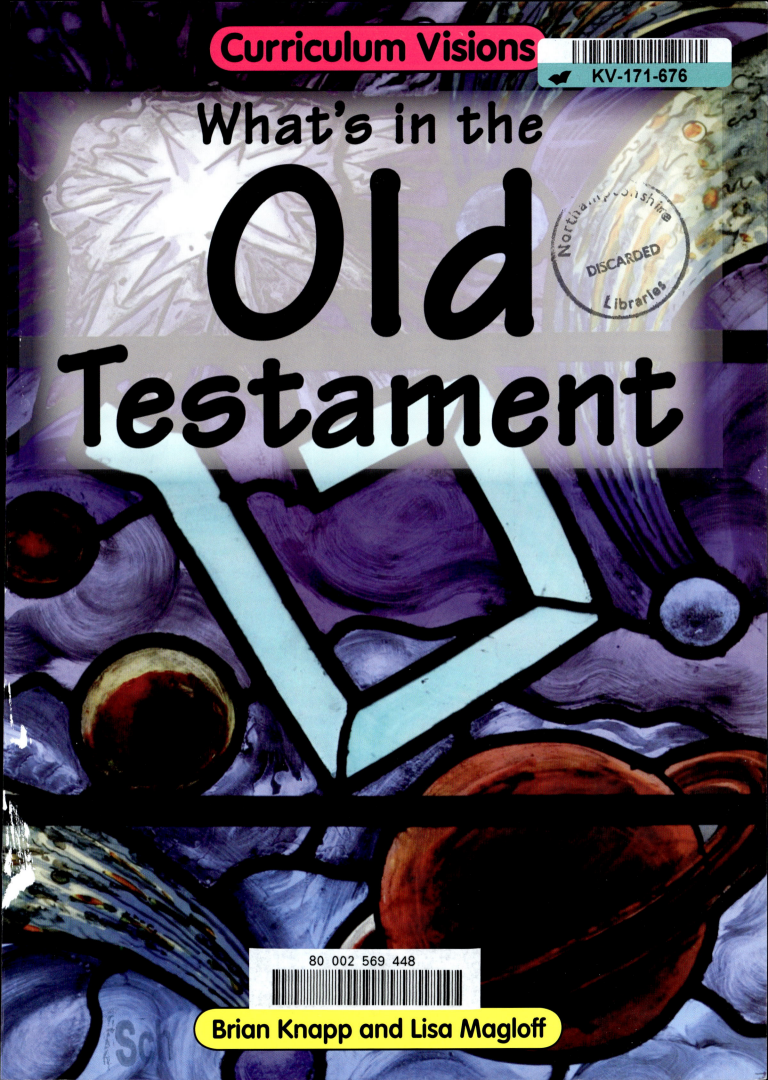

Curriculum Visions

What's in the Old Testament

Brian Knapp and Lisa Magloff

Glossary

Look out for these words as you go through the book. They are shown using CAPITALS.

APOCRYPHA This word means 'hidden' and refers to writings that some traditions do not consider to be part of the Bible.

BABYLON The capital of the ancient Babylonian empire which captured Israel and placed the Israelites in slavery.

COMMANDMENT A command or order. There are many commandments in the Old Testament, but the most important are the Ten Commandments.

DEUTERONOMY This is the fifth book of the Bible. The word Deuteronomy means second law and this book contains a second telling of the laws given to the Jewish people by God.

EXODUS One of the first five books of the Bible. The word Exodus means 'way out' and this book tells the story of how God saved the Jewish people from slavery in Egypt.

GENESIS The first book of the Bible. Genesis means beginning.

HEBREW The language spoken by the ancient Israelites. Modern day Israelis also speak a more modern version of Hebrew. The ancient Jewish people were also called the Hebrew people, or the Israelites.

ISRAEL The name that God gave to Jacob. Israel is also the name of the land that was promised to the Jewish people by God in the Old Testament. This is the Promised Land where Jacob (Israel) and his descendants settled. Ancient Israel was not exactly the same shape or size as modern Israel.

ISRAELITES The descendants of Jacob (Israel). This word is also used to refer to the Jewish people.

JESUS CHRIST was born with the name Jesus of Nazareth. After he began preaching, people called him the Messiah, or the anointed one. The word Christ is a Greek word which means 'the Messiah'. So, Christ is a title and Jesus Christ means Jesus the Messiah.

JUDGES Leaders of ancient Israel. Their story is told in the Book of Judges.

LEVITICUS One of the first five books of the Bible. In ancient times, the group of Jews called the Levites were the only ones allowed to perform many religious rituals. This book contains many rules and laws for conducting these rituals.

MESSIAH The person told about in the Bible who will save the Jewish people. Christians believe Jesus was the Messiah and that he came to save all people.

MIDDLE EAST A modern name for the part of the world where Israel and Egypt are located.

NEW TESTAMENT The part of the Bible that tells the story of Jesus and the apostles.

NUMBERS One of the first five books of the Bible. It is called Numbers because it contains a list, or numbering, of the Israelites who wandered in the desert after fleeing Egypt.

OLD TESTAMENT The part of the Bible that tells the history of the Jewish people from the beginning of time until before Jesus was born.

PROMISED LAND The land that God promised to the descendants of Abraham. In the Bible, this land was called Canaan. The country of ancient Israel included Canaan.

PROPHET A person who has a special relationship with God. Prophets can often interpret the will of God so that people can understand it.

PROVERB A short phrase that tells a moral or lesson.

SACRIFICE To give up something that is important to you, or to kill an animal for a religious rite. In ancient times, Jews would often sacrifice animals to God.

SAVIOUR Another way of describing Jesus. A saviour is someone who rescues or 'saves' another person. Christians believe that Jesus was sent to save people from their sins, so he is called 'the Saviour'.

TEN COMMANDMENTS The most important of the commandments (laws) that God gave to Moses.

TORAH The Jewish word for the first five books of the Bible. In Judaism, the Torah is hand-written onto a parchment scroll by a specially-trained scribe.

Contents

How the Old Testament
        came to be 4

The Old Testament story 6

Genesis: the creation 12

Adam and Eve 14

Noah and the flood...................... 16

The story of Abraham 18

Joseph in the land of Egypt 20

Moses and the commandments... 22

The prophet Isaiah 24

The prophet Daniel 26

Psalms 28

Proverbs 30

Index.. 32

(Title page) A stained glass window showing the creation of
Heaven and Earth. *(Right)* God gave Moses two stone tablets
containing the Ten Commandments.

How the Old Testament came to be

The Old Testament is a collection of writings dating from between 1,500 and 400 years before Christian times.

The word testament means 'agreement'. The **OLD TESTAMENT** is the name used by Christians for the collection of sacred writings made by Jews (who are also called **ISRAELITES** in the Old Testament) in the time before **JESUS CHRIST**. It tells of a special agreement between the Jewish people and God and of the creation of the nation of ancient **ISRAEL**.

The name of the Old Testament

Christians use the words Old Testament to describe this part of the Bible because they believe that a new agreement (**NEW TESTAMENT**) was made with God through Jesus Christ.

Jewish people do not use the word Old Testament, but instead call these books the Jewish Bible or the Tanak. Tanak is a **HEBREW** word which is formed of the first letters of the three parts of the Jewish Bible: Torah (Law), Nevi'im (Prophets) and Ketuvim (Writings).

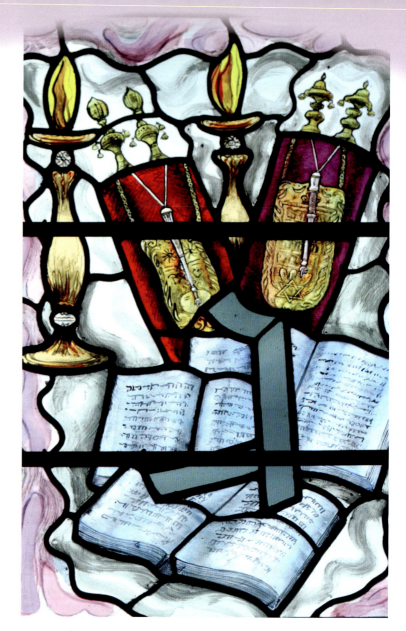

▲ This stained glass shows the books of the Jewish Bible. The first five books of the Bible were originally written on **TORAH** scrolls, like those shown on page 5.

Collecting the writings into a book

The Old Testament is a collection of many types of writings. There are prophesies, history, instructions directly from God, the teachings of wise men, legends, songs and poems.

Most of the Old Testament was written in Hebrew over a period of hundreds of years. Some of the books were written many generations after the events they talk about happened.

Weblink: www.CurriculumVisions.com

For example, the story of Abraham was not written down until hundreds of years after it happened.

The first books that would become the Old Testament were written down on parchment scrolls and passed on as sacred writings for hundreds of years. Over time, as new events happened, new books were added. Eventually, all of the books were collected together into one big book, the Old Testament.

Did the stories really happen?

This is about the hardest question when you start looking at how the Old Testament came to be. There is no real historical evidence that Noah, Abraham, Isaac, Jacob and others really existed. So it is a question of faith. You either have to believe in the stories because the Old Testament says so, or you believe that the stories were written as legends or as a way to inspire others.

But even if the stories are not strictly accurate, they do describe ways of life that we know were common in ancient times. Where we can check the books of the Old Testament against other sources of history, they do tend to agree. So the settings are probably accurate. But this does not help us to know if the stories are really true. That is a question of faith.

When you write something, you do it with a certain point of view. You can't help this, and it can affect the way you report things. For example, you will know that newspaper reporters covering the same event make that event sound quite different. The people who wrote the Old Testament also wrote in a way that was affected by their life and times.

Some people think that most of the stories in the Old Testament are legend, but many believe they were probably centred around real people. What you need to ask yourself is this: has the message God intended come through loud and clear? People who believe in the Old Testament would all say yes to this, no matter what they think of the details.

▼ A Torah scroll being held up in a synagogue.

5

The Old Testament Story

The Old Testament tells the story of how God revealed Himself to the Jewish people.

The Old Testament tells the story of how God has revealed himself to people on Earth. This includes telling the story of how the ancient state of Israel came to be and the history of the ancient Jewish people.

This is a long story and includes a lot of history and detail. For example, one whole book describes how to perform ancient worship rituals, who was allowed to be one of the ancient priests, and how they should behave. Other parts of the Old Testament contain laws that people should live by, and long lists of family trees. Some of the books of the Old Testament tell the same story, but in slightly different ways.

To help you understand what you read in the Old Testament, here is an outline of what you will find.

Genesis: The beginning

GENESIS begins with the creation of the world by God. The first 11 chapters of this book include the stories of Adam and Eve, Cain and Abel, the Tower of Babel, and Noah and the flood.

The rest of the book (chapters 12–50) tells the story of Abraham and his children. God promises Abraham that he will be the leader of a great nation if Abraham agrees to worship only God.

Abraham agrees and goes through many trials before coming to the land that God promised to him (the **PROMISED LAND**), called Canaan.

The book then describes what happens to the children and grandchildren of Abraham. It ends when Abraham's grandson Jacob (who is renamed Israel by God) and his 12 sons and their families all flee to Egypt to escape famine.

Exodus: Slavery and deliverance

As the book of **EXODUS** begins, we find out how the children of Israel (Jacob), the Jewish people, are made into slaves while they are in Egypt.

Moses becomes the leader of the Israelites and God promises to deliver them from slavery and lead them back to the Promised Land. God sends 12 plagues to Egypt, and parts the Red Sea. Moses leads the Israelites out of slavery and into the desert.

In the desert, God gives Moses the **TEN COMMANDMENTS** and makes a new agreement with the Israelites that He will protect them if they agree to worship only Him. At first the Israelites do not agree and begin to worship a golden calf, but then they repent and agree to follow God.

Weblink: www.CurriculumVisions.com

THE OLD TESTAMENT

Genesis
Exodus
Leviticus
Numbers
Deuteronomy

The Law

◄▼ Here are the books of the Old Testament, in order.

Joshua
Judges
Ruth
1 Samuel
2 Samuel
1 Kings
2 Kings
1 Chronicles
2 Chronicles
Ezra
Nehemiah
Esther

Historical books

Job
Psalms
Proverbs
Ecclesiastes
Song of Songs

Wisdom books

Isaiah
Jeremiah
Lamentations
Ezekiel
Daniel

Major prophets

Hosea
Joel
Amos
Obadiah
Jonah
Micah
Nahum
Habakkuk
Zephaniah
Haggai
Zechariah
Malachi

Minor prophets

Weblink: www.CurriculumVisions.com

Numbers, Leviticus and Deuteronomy: in the desert

The book of **NUMBERS** tells the story of how the Israelites spent 40 years wandering in the desert before they reached the Promised Land. Numbers also describes the battles that the Israelites fought in order to conquer the Promised Land (Canaan) before they could live there.

In the book of **LEVITICUS**, Moses writes down all of the rules and laws which the Israelites must follow. These include how to conduct worship, what to do on the Sabbath (Holy Day), who may be a priest and lead worship, how to make offerings, how to build an altar for conducting worship and many other things.

The book of **DEUTERONOMY** begins on the bank of the Jordan River. As the Israelites are about to cross and enter the Promised Land, Moses retells the story of their journey and reminds the Israelites of their promises to obey God's laws. At the end of the book, Moses blesses the Israelites and then dies. Joshua takes over as leader of the Israelite people and leads them across the Jordan River and into the Promised Land.

Historical books: the time of kings

The next 12 books of the Old Testament describe the history of ancient Israel. This begins with the book of Joshua, which tells the story of how Joshua led the Israelites across the Jordan River, conquered the land of Canaan and divided it up among the 12 families of the sons of Israel (Jacob).

For many generations the Israelites defended their land against outside attacks. At first, the land is ruled by men called **JUDGES**, but they do not do a good job and the people demand a king. Under the kings Saul, David and Solomon, the Kingdom of ancient Israel is founded.

Saul becomes the first king over Israel, but Saul's leadership creates serious problems and leaves the kingdom in a weakened state. After Saul's death, David becomes king and he makes Israel into a stronger country.

David is succeeded by Solomon, who makes Jerusalem the capital and builds The Temple there. When Solomon dies the kingdom splits apart into a Northern Kingdom (called Israel) and a Southern Kingdom (called Judah). The Northern Kingdom is eventually destroyed by its neighbours. The Southern Kingdom is conquered by the Babylonian empire in 587 BC, and the Jews are brought to **BABYLON** as captives.

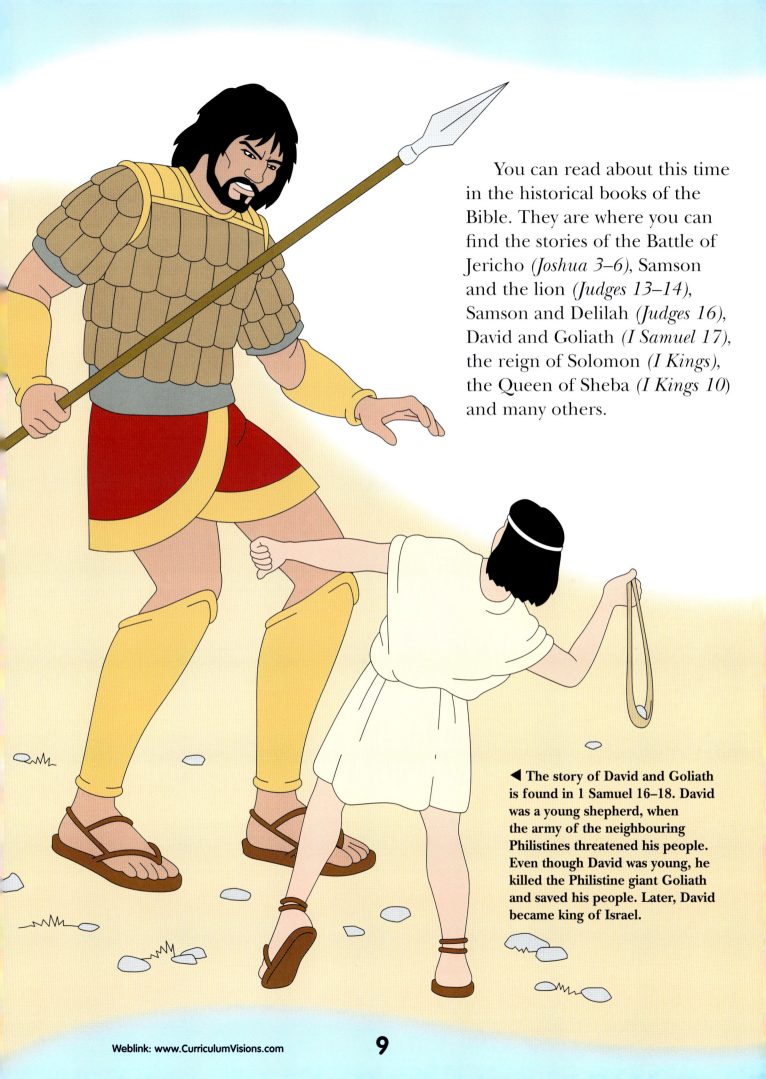

You can read about this time in the historical books of the Bible. They are where you can find the stories of the Battle of Jericho (*Joshua 3–6*), Samson and the lion (*Judges 13–14*), Samson and Delilah (*Judges 16*), David and Goliath (*I Samuel 17*), the reign of Solomon (*I Kings*), the Queen of Sheba (*I Kings 10*) and many others.

◄ **The story of David and Goliath is found in 1 Samuel 16–18. David was a young shepherd, when the army of the neighbouring Philistines threatened his people. Even though David was young, he killed the Philistine giant Goliath and saved his people. Later, David became king of Israel.**

Prophets: Captivity and return

These 17 books largely tell the story of how Israel was conquered by the Babylonian empire, and what happened to the Jewish people after this. These books contain many stories of suffering and exile, but also of hope. The writers were writing at a time of great suffering for the Jewish people. So, they are also trying to explain why this suffering is happening and to give assurance that God still loves the Jewish people.

Eventually the Babylonians were beaten by the Persians and the Jews were allowed to return to their homeland to rebuild Jerusalem.

The Old Testament closes at about 400 BC when all of the lands of the **MIDDLE EAST** came under the Greek rule of Alexander the Great and then fell under the control of the Romans.

In these books you can find the stories of Daniel in the lions' den *(Daniel 6)*, how Esther saves the Jews *(Esther)*, the rebuilding of Jerusalem *(Ezra 1, Nehemiah 1–8)*, Jonah and the whale *(Jonah 1–4)* and many more.

▶ The Jewish festival of Purim celebrates how Esther saved the Jewish people during their captivity in Babylon. Purim is a fun and happy festival and is often celebrated with fetes, fancy dress and special foods.

Weblink: www.CurriculumVisions.com

The Wisdom writings

This part of the Old Testament is made up of five books, called Psalms, Job, Proverbs, Ecclesiastes and the Song of Songs. All of these are writings in praise of God.

The book of Job describes a god-fearing man, Job. Satan challenges God to test Job's faith. God then tests Job by making him suffer terribly: his children die and he loses everything he has. Job asks himself why good people suffer and he questions God's justice. Eventually, God speaks to Job and Job repents for ever questioning God.

The Book of Psalms was originally written as a prayer book to be used during worship. It contains poems and prayers in praise of God that were meant to be sung as part of worship.

The **PROVERBS** in the Book of Proverbs were written in order to teach important lessons in a very simple way. The proverbs give advice for correct behaviour, such as encouraging hard work and honesty, and avoiding pride and arrogance.

Ecclesiastes means 'teacher', and the author of this book writes about how we cannot really know the wisdom of God and must rely instead on faith to give life meaning.

The Song of Songs is also called the Song of Solomon, because it was written by King Solomon. It is a long and beautiful poem about love and the love of God.

The Apocrypha

Did you know that not all Bibles have the same number of Old Testament books? The Jewish Bible contains 24 books, the Protestant Old Testament, 39 books, the Eastern Orthodox, 43 books, and the Roman Catholic, 46 books.

In some cases, the books are simply divided up differently. For example, the book in the Jewish Bible called "The Twelve", which contains the writings of 12 prophets, is split out into 12 separate books in the Protestant Bible.

The additional books in the Orthodox and Roman Catholic Bibles include material that Jews and Protestants do not accept as sacred. They put them in a separate category called the **APOCRYPHA**.

The nine books of the Apocrypha were written between the fourth century BC and the time of Jesus. They mostly tell stories of a time when Jews were held captive in Babylonia.

On the following pages, you can learn more about some of the parts of the Old Testament in depth.

Genesis: the creation

The first part of the Book of Genesis describes the creation of the universe.

The Old Testament begins by describing how God created the universe and everything in it:

> *In the beginning God created the Heavens and the Earth. (Genesis 1:1)*

(The words Heavens and Earth are used because there is no Hebrew word for universe.)

The idea that the universe was empty of everything except for God is given in the second line:

> *Now the Earth was formless and empty, darkness was over the surface of the deep, and the Spirit of God was hovering over the waters. (Genesis 1:2)*

(The word waters is used here to mean space.)

After this, the rest of the first chapter of Genesis describes how God created everything in six days. Many people think six days is used to mean 'a long time'.

The first six days

On the first day, God created light, day and night:

> *And God said, "Let there be light," and there was light.*
>
> *God saw that the light was good, and He separated the light from the darkness.*
>
> *God called the light "day," and the darkness he called "night." And there was evening, and there was morning – the first day. (Genesis 1:2–4)*

On the second day, God created Heaven *(1:6–8)*, the space that separates the Earth from the rest of the universe.

On day 3, God created dry land and the seas and plants *(1:9–13)*. On the fourth day, God created the Sun, Moon, stars and the seasons *(1:14–19)*. On day five God created the birds and the animals that live in the water *(1:20–23)*.

Weblink: www.CurriculumVisions.com

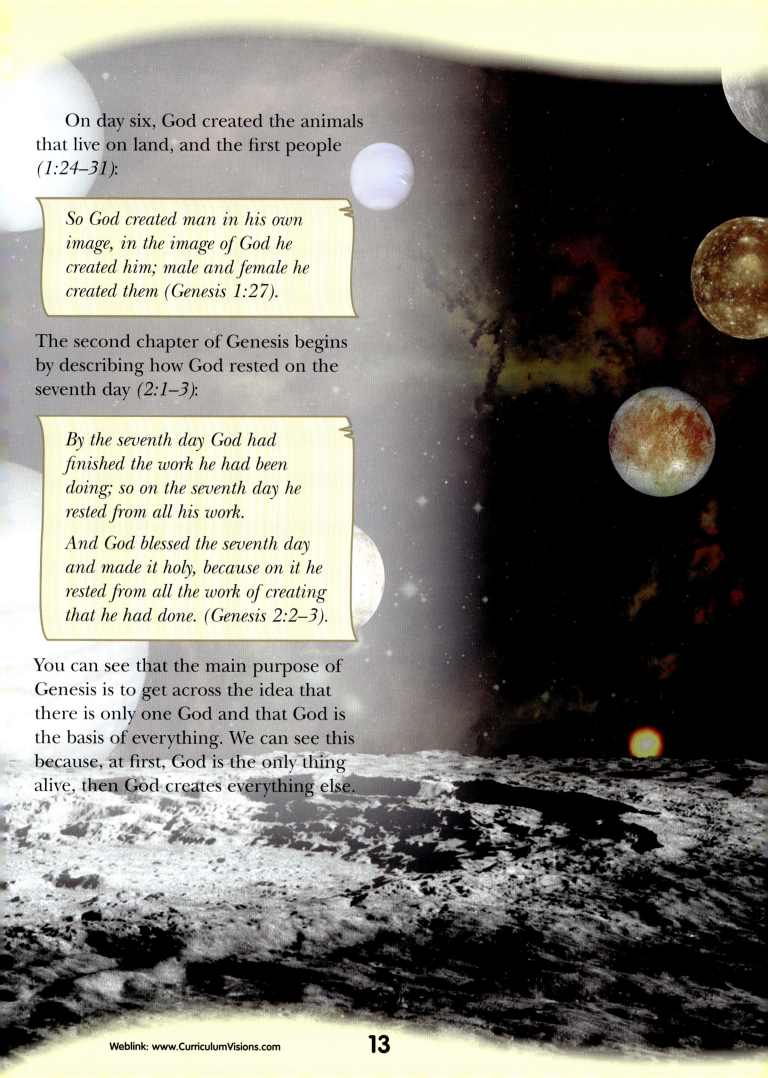

On day six, God created the animals that live on land, and the first people *(1:24–31)*:

> *So God created man in his own image, in the image of God he created him; male and female he created them (Genesis 1:27).*

The second chapter of Genesis begins by describing how God rested on the seventh day *(2:1–3)*:

> *By the seventh day God had finished the work he had been doing; so on the seventh day he rested from all his work.*
>
> *And God blessed the seventh day and made it holy, because on it he rested from all the work of creating that he had done. (Genesis 2:2–3).*

You can see that the main purpose of Genesis is to get across the idea that there is only one God and that God is the basis of everything. We can see this because, at first, God is the only thing alive, then God creates everything else.

Adam and Eve

After the creation, the Book of Genesis tells us about the first people.

The second and third chapters of Genesis tell the story of the creation of the first people: Adam and Eve.

First God creates Adam and puts him in the Garden of Eden. In the middle of the Garden, God puts the Tree of Knowledge and God tells Adam that he can eat anything in the Garden except the fruit of the Tree of Knowledge.

> *The LORD God formed the man from the dust of the ground and breathed into his nostrils the breath of life, and the man became a living being.*
>
> *Now the LORD God had planted a garden in the east, in Eden; and there he put the man he had formed. (Genesis 2:7–8)*

Then, because God does not want Adam to be alone, he creates Eve to keep Adam company.

One day an evil serpent convinces Eve to eat the fruit of the Tree of Knowledge, and Eve then convinces Adam to eat the fruit. Because they disobeyed God, Adam and Eve are thrown out of the Garden of Eden forever.

▲ This stained glass window shows the Tree of Knowledge in the Garden of Eden. You can also see the serpent in the tree.

They must now work to grow their own food and suffer sorrow and pain:

> *By the sweat of your brow*
> *you will eat your food*
> *until you return to the ground,*
> *since from it you were taken;*
> *for dust you are and to dust you*
> *will return. (Genesis 3:19)*

The meaning of the story

In Hebrew, the word Adam means 'mankind'. It does not mean a male person by the name of Adam. So one way of looking at this story is as a story of all mankind; mankind was originally innocent and did not know bad from good and so could not commit sins. When the fruit of the tree is eaten mankind (Adam and Eve) then discover that there is a thing called sin and so they are now capable of doing bad things.

The serpent that causes Adam and Eve to disobey God and eat the fruit is a way of saying that we all have a bad character inside us. If we listen to this bad character then we can commit sins.

All of this is a way of explaining why people have to work hard in life in order to survive, and why there is suffering and sorrow in life.

Cain and Abel (Genesis 4:1–24)

After Adam and Eve leave the Garden of Eden, they have two sons, Cain and Abel. Cain is a farmer and Abel is a shepherd.

Cain and Abel both make offerings to God. Abel SACRIFICES his best sheep and Cain gives some grain and fruit, but not his best. Because Abel gave his best sheep, God prefers the offerings of Abel. This makes Cain jealous and he kills Abel.

> *Now Cain said to his brother Abel, "Let's go out to the field." And while they were in the field, Cain attacked his brother Abel and killed him.*
>
> *Then the LORD said to Cain, "Where is your brother Abel?"*
>
> *"I don't know," he replied. "Am I my brother's keeper?" (Genesis 4:8–9)*

As a punishment, God banishes Cain from his land and from God's presence.

In this story we can see that outside the Garden of Eden it is much easier to be tempted by bad feelings, such as jealousy, and commit sins like murder.

Noah and the flood

God decides to wipe the world clean of the sinful and start all over again.

In this part of the Old Testament, a worldwide flood occurs and everyone is drowned except for the people in Noah's Ark. There is no evidence for this flood at all, but the meaning is quite clear: if you disobey God's will, you can expect the worst.

Weblink: www.CurriculumVisions.com

A sinful world

The story of Noah is told in Genesis chapters 6–9. It begins by telling us that for many generations people had not followed the will of God and that the world had become a sinful place. This made God very sad and he decided to destroy everything he had created. However, God decided to save one good man, Noah, and his family.

So God told Noah that he intended to wipe the world clean of sin and start again. Noah was told to build a boat which was large enough to hold at least two of every kind of animal in the world (a male and female). This is the boat that was called the Ark.

The flood

When the Ark was completed and all of the animals were loaded in, the sky turned grey and it rained. The Bible says that it rained for 40 days and 40 nights, until everything on Earth was covered with water. The flood lasted for 150 days, and then the Ark came to rest on the very top of Mt Ararat. Here, the numbers 40 and 150 might mean 40 days and 150 days, or they may simply mean 'a long time'.

A new beginning

Noah wanted to know if it was safe to leave the Ark. First he sent a raven to find some dry ground, but it only flew back and forth. Then Noah sent out a dove, but as there was no dry land it flew back. Then he sent it again, and it came back with a leaf in its mouth, meaning that plants were growing again. The last time he sent it out it never came back, meaning it had found a place to live. This was 300 days after the start of the flood.

Now God told Noah that he could leave the Ark. Noah's family, and all of the animals, found new homes in the world God had washed clean.

Thanking God

The first thing Noah did after leaving the Ark was to build a stone altar and make offerings to God. God was pleased with what Noah had done and told Noah that he will never again destroy the world with a flood.

> "Never again will I curse the ground because of man... And never again will I destroy all living creatures, as I have done. As long as the Earth endures, seedtime and harvest, cold and heat, summer and winter, day and night will never cease."
> (Genesis 6:20–22)

The message of the story of Noah and the flood is clear. God can destroy everything if He wishes, and sin will always be punished. But God accepts that all people are capable of sin and He will be merciful and spare people who are good and who worship God.

The story of Abraham

This story in the Book of Genesis tells us how Abraham became the founder of the Israelite people and about the Promised Land.

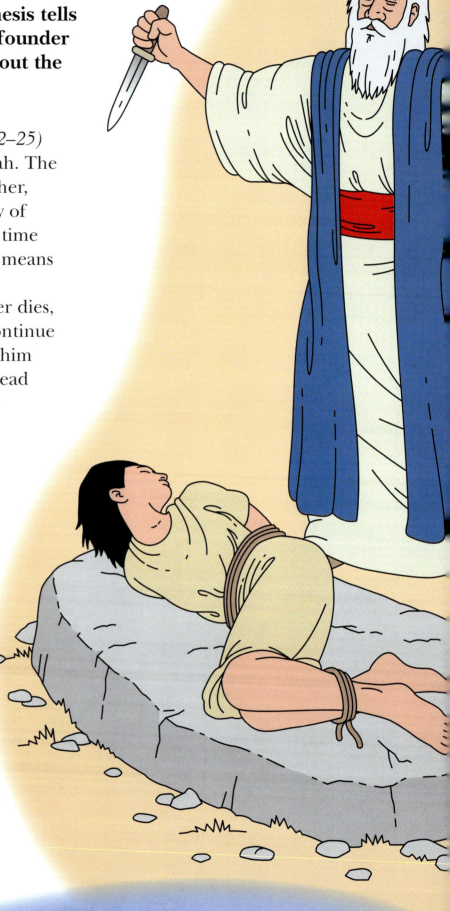

The story of Abraham (*Genesis 12–25*) begins long after the time of Noah. The story begins when Abraham's father, Terah, leaves his home in the city of Ur (in modern-day Iraq). At this time Abraham is called Abram, which means 'blessed father'.

Sometime after Abram's father dies, God tells Abram that if he will continue the journey, then God will make him the father of a great nation and lead him to a great land (Canaan, the Promised Land).

Abram obeys God and God leads Abram to Canaan. Abram settles with his family in Canaan, but he wonders how God will make him the father of a great nation because he is already an old man and he has no children.

When Abram is 99 years old and his wife Sarah is 90, God promises the couple a son and renames Abram as Abraham ('father of many').

Sarah laughed when she heard God say that she would have a child. As a result, God told them to name their child Isaac, which means laughter.

Weblink: www.CurriculumVisions.com

◀ God tested Abraham's faith by asking him to sacrifice his son Isaac on an altar. At this time, it was common practice to sacrifice animals to God in this way. Abraham prepared to sacrifice Isaac, but at the last moment God told him he could sacrifice a ram (a male sheep) instead.

Abraham's sacrifice

One day, when Isaac was still a boy, God told Abraham to **SACRIFICE** Isaac on an altar. Abraham agreed, but at the last moment, God stopped him (*Genesis 22:1–18*) and told him to sacrifice a sheep instead. This was a test of faith, and Abraham had passed.

Abraham's grandson, Jacob

The next part of Genesis (*25–33*) tells the story of Abraham's son, Isaac.

When Isaac grew up he married Rebecca and they had twin sons, Jacob and Esau. Isaac loved Esau best, but Rebecca tricked Isaac into letting Jacob inherit all his possessions instead of Esau. To avoid his brother's anger, Jacob left his home in Canaan and travelled to Haran (in modern-day Iraq). There, Jacob worked hard for 14 years and married Rachel.

Eventually, Jacob decided to return home to Canaan. He was very worried that his brother would kill his family, so he divided them into two groups and sent each group in a different direction. He also chose the best of his herds to give as a gift to his brother.

That night, Jacob sat alone by the river, to think about his life. Suddenly, a stranger appeared and began to argue with him. When the Sun rose, the stranger said, "Now it is morning and I must leave. From now on your name shall not be Jacob but Israel." Jacob realised that he had been arguing with God!

The next morning Jacob bowed down in front of his brother seven times and asked his forgiveness. Esau forgave him and they are reunited.

Eventually, Jacob had 12 sons and a daughter: Gad, Asher, Reuben, Simeon, Levi, Judah, Issachar, Zebulun, Dan, Naphtali, Joseph, Benjamin and Dinah.

In the story, Jacob did a very bad thing when he agreed with his mother to deceive his father. But he realised his mistake, worked hard for many years and eventually asked for his brother's forgiveness. The story is telling us that even when we do bad things, we can make them better by repenting (apologising) and leading a good life.

Joseph in the land of Egypt

This story tells of the trials of Joseph and how eventually the Israelites found themselves in Egypt.

The story of how the children of Jacob (Israel) and their families ended up living in Egypt is told in Genesis 37–50. The story begins where the story of Jacob (Israel) left off.

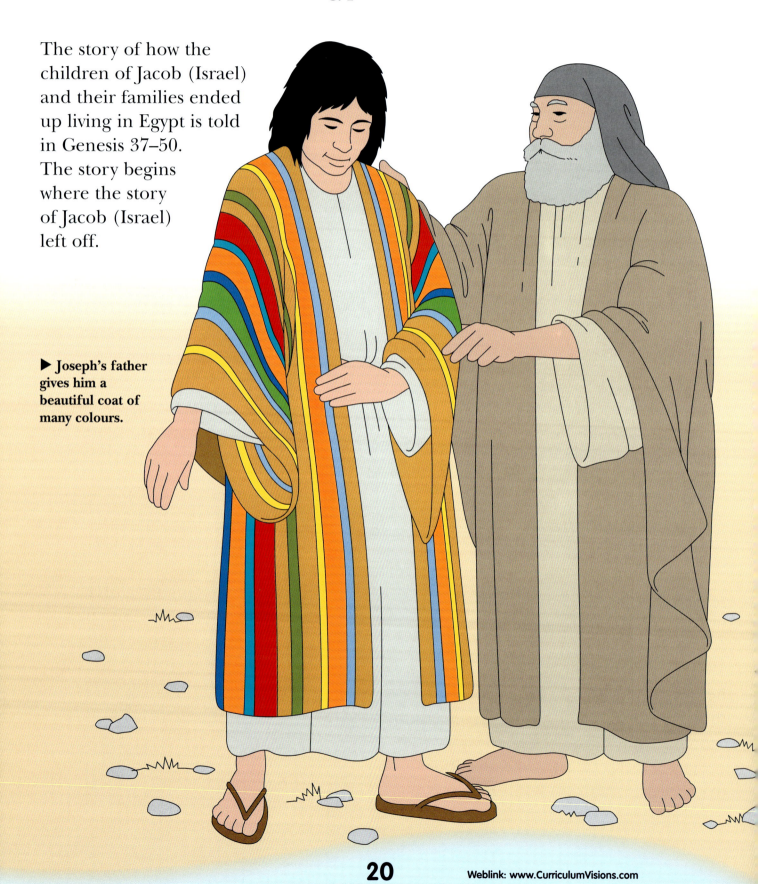

► Joseph's father gives him a beautiful coat of many colours.

Joseph is sold into slavery

Jacob had 12 sons who were each head of a tribe – the 12 tribes of Israel, but Joseph was Jacob's favourite son.

Joseph's brothers hated him because he was their father's favourite. One day, Joseph told his brothers about a dream he had: "I dreamt that we were in the fields at harvest, tying up sheaves of corn. My sheaf of corn stood upright, while your sheaves bowed down to it."

Later, Joseph told his brothers another dream: "I dreamt that the Sun and the Moon in the sky and eleven stars were all bowing down to me."

Both dreams showed Joseph as the leader of his family, and when Joseph's brothers heard these dreams they became very angry and jealous. They tricked their father into thinking that Joseph was dead, and then sold Joseph into slavery in Egypt.

Joseph in Egypt

In Egypt, Joseph became known as a person who was able to explain people's dreams. One day, the Pharaoh had a very strange dream that no one could explain.

Finally, Joseph was sent for and he explained that the dream meant there would be seven years of plenty, followed by seven years of drought. He advised the Pharaoh to store grain from the plentiful harvests to be used during the famine. The Pharaoh was so impressed with this that he freed Joseph and promoted him to a position of great power, second only to the Pharaoh.

Joseph then set about storing Egypt's excess grain. When the famine arrived, as Joseph had predicted, there was enough grain for everyone. There was so much grain that people from the surrounding countries came to Egypt to buy grain.

Some of the people who came to buy grain were Joseph's brothers, the same brothers who had sold him into slavery. They were very surprised to find that Joseph was now wealthy and powerful. Joseph forgave his brothers and so they and all their families (the Israelites) moved to Egypt to escape the famine in Canaan.

The meaning of the story

This story continues the story of Abraham and his family, but it also teaches important lessons.

Even though Joseph's brothers sold him into slavery, Joseph helped them after he became powerful in Egypt. This teaches us that family is more important than anything else.

This story also prepares us for the story of Moses and the Exodus, which is told in the next book of the Old Testament.

Moses and the commandments

The Book of Exodus tells the story of Moses and how he led the Israelites out of Egypt and of how God made a new covenant with the Jewish people.

The story of Moses begins with the Israelites in Egypt suffering a change in fortune.

The Israelites have lived in Egypt for a long time and had become wealthy and powerful. But now Joseph is long dead and there is a new Pharaoh on the throne. This Pharaoh does not like the Israelites and he has them all turned into slaves.

Then, the Pharaoh commands that every male Israelite newborn child should be killed. One young couple hide their newborn son for three months. But when the boy grows too big to hide any longer, his mother puts him in the river in a basket. This baby is found by the Pharaoh's daughter, who decides to keep him. She names him Moses, which means 'to be taken out' (of the river).

Moses is brought up as an Egyptian, but his mother becomes his nurse and as he grows up she reminds him that he is an Israelite. One day, Moses comes across an Egyptian beating up an Israelite. Moses kills the attacker and then flees from Egypt.

In the desert, God appears to Moses as a burning bush and tells him to return to Egypt and ask the Pharaoh to let the Israelites return to Canaan.

The Pharaoh refuses Moses' request and so God sends ten plagues to Egypt (see below). After the last plague, in which all the Egyptian first-born sons are killed, the Pharaoh agrees to let the Israelites leave. God parts the Red Sea so that the Israelites can cross to the Sinai desert.

The Plagues of Egypt

Plague 1	The waters of the River Nile turn to blood.
Plague 2	The land of Egypt is covered with frogs.
Plague 3	A plague of gnats covered the land.
Plague 4	A plague of flies.
Plague 5	All of the cattle get diseases.
Plague 6	The people became covered in boils.
Plague 7	Hailstorms flatten all of the crops in the fields.
Plague 8	Locusts eat all the crops.
Plague 9	The plague of darkness. God caused total darkness for three days.
Plague 10	The curse of the first-born. God sent an angel to kill all of the Egyptian first-born. He told the Israelites to put a dab of lamb's blood on their doors, so the angel of death would know who was an Israelite and would not kill anyone in that house.

Exodus

In the Sinai desert, God looks after the Israelites by sending water, quails and manna (bread) from Heaven, but some people complain that life in the desert was worse than slavery.

Weblink: www.CurriculumVisions.com

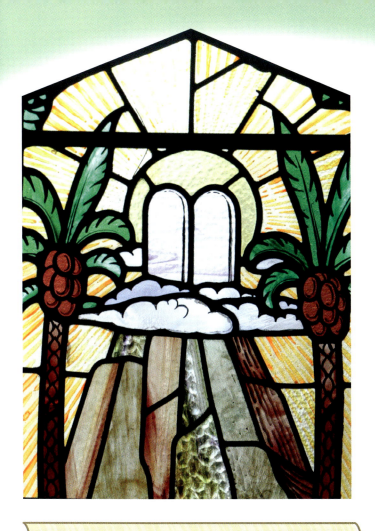

The Ten Commandments:

❶ **You shall have no other gods before me.**

❷ **You shall not make any carved images.**

❸ **You shall not misuse the name of your God.**

❹ **Remember the Sabbath day, to keep it holy.**

❺ **Honour your father and mother.**

❻ **You shall not kill.**

❼ **You shall not commit adultery (having sexual relations with someone you are not married to).**

❽ **You shall not steal.**

❾ **You shall not bear false witness.**

❿ **You shall not covet (want things belonging to other people).**

After three months, they reach Mt Sinai, and Moses goes up on the mountain to pray. While on Mt Sinai, God gives Moses the Ten Commandments, engraved on two stone tablets.

But while Moses is on the mountain, the Israelites become worried and lose faith. They build a golden calf and begin to worship it instead of God. When Moses comes down from the mountain and sees the calf, he smashes the tablets God had given him, but he also begs God to forgive the people.

God does punish the people at first, but he also gives Moses two more stone tablets with the commandments on them and instructions for how to worship Him.

The meaning of the story

In this story you can see that Moses is destined to save the Israelites from slavery.

Even though the Israelites lose their faith in the desert, they repent, and so God renews the agreement that he made with Abraham to lead them to the Promised Land if they will worship only God. This time, God also gives them laws (commandments) to use in their worship.

◀ The Ten Commandments. Above these is a stained glass window showing the tablets containing the commandments on Mt Sinai.

The prophet Isaiah

Isaiah was one of the great prophets of the Old Testament who foresaw the coming of the Messiah.

Isaiah is one of the most important books of the part of the Bible called Prophets. A **PROPHET** is someone who has a special relationship with God, and who God speaks through. Many of the prophets could make predictions, called prophecies, about the future.

Many of the prophecies in Isaiah have to do with the coming of a **MESSIAH** to save the Jewish people. These prophecies are important for Christians, who believe that Isaiah foretold the coming of Jesus Christ.

Who was Isaiah?

Isaiah lived in about the eighth century BC. He came from Judah and lived in Jerusalem. Isaiah wrote at about the same time as the prophets Amos, Hosea and Micah. At this time, the Jewish Kingdoms of Israel and Judah were under threat from their neighbours, the Assyrian Kingdom and the Babylonian Kingdom.

Isaiah and the other prophets of this time criticised the way the priests ran the religion and felt that people had become sinful and had strayed from the path set out by God. Isaiah and the other prophets see it as their duty to warn people of what will happen if they continue to fail God's **COMMANDMENTS**.

Isaiah tells of a time when Jerusalem will be conquered and the people sent away in captivity. But he also writes that the people will be saved by a king who is descended from David and who will reign over the Lord's Kingdom on Earth.

Here are some of Isaiah's prophecies. Some of them may already be familiar to you.

The Messiah

Isaiah tells us that he heard the call from God to become a divine messenger. In Chapter 6, Isaiah says:

> *In the year that King Uzziah died, I saw the Lord seated on a throne, high and exalted… (6:1)*
>
> *Then I heard the voice of the Lord saying, "Whom shall I send? And who will go for us?" And I said, "Here am I. Send me!" (Isaiah 6:8)*

Isaiah then explains that the people have forgotten God's laws, and condemns the sinfulness and rebelliousness of the nation and foretells a time of judgement.

 Weblink: www.CurriculumVisions.com

> *"Come now, let us reason together,"*
> *says the LORD.*
> *"Though your sins are like scarlet,*
> *they shall be as white as snow;*
> *though they are red as crimson,*
> *they shall be like wool.*
> *(Isaiah 1:18)*

After describing how Israel will be overthrown and the people taken into captivity, Isaiah describes how they will be freed and return to Jerusalem. Later, he tells how God will send a **SAVIOUR** to Jerusalem:

> *For to us a child is born,*
> *to us a son is given,*
> *and the government will be on his shoulders.*
> *And he will be called Wonderful Counsellor, Mighty God, Everlasting Father, Prince of Peace. (Isaiah 9:6)*

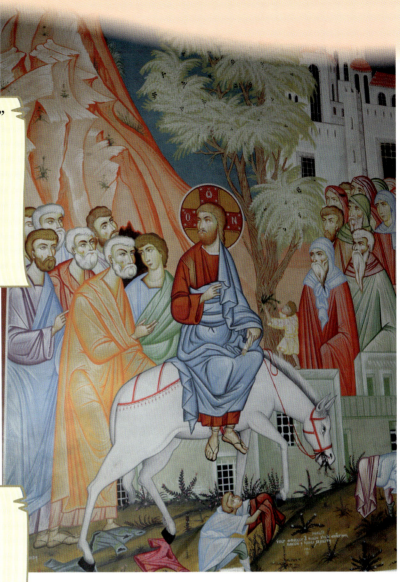

▲ Jesus Christ, the Saviour, entering Jerusalem, as foretold by Isaiah.

Isaiah also describes how the Saviour will suffer and die to save mankind:

> *With righteousness he will judge the needy,*
> *with justice he will give decisions for the poor of the Earth.*
> *He will strike the Earth with the rod of his mouth;*
> *with the breath of his lips he will slay the wicked.*
> *(Isaiah 11:4)*

> *"He was despised and rejected by men, a man of sorrows, and familiar with suffering.... But he was pierced for our transgressions, he was crushed for our iniquities; the punishment that brought us peace was upon him, and by his wounds we are healed."*
> *(Isaiah 53:3,5)*

The prophet Daniel

The Book of Daniel tells about how the prophet Daniel stood by his faith in difficult times and about the coming of the Messiah.

The Book of Daniel tells the story of Daniel, one of the royal family of Judah who is taken captive when the Babylonians attack Judah in about 606 BC. Daniel lived into his 90s, through the reign of several kings of Babylon.

This book was written during a time when Jews were suffering and so its purpose was to give people encouragement in difficult times, and to let them know that God is in control of history and will make everything better. It partly prophesies events just about to happen, but also tells about the coming of the Messiah in future centuries.

Nebuchadnezzar, king of Babylon

This part of Daniel's story tells of how eventually the mighty Nebuchadnezzar, king of Babylon, was brought to see the power of God through the way that he persecuted Daniel.

The first part of the story tells of how Daniel was sent as a captive to work in the court of the king of Babylon. The captives were ordered to eat the same food as the king, which was forbidden for Jews. But Daniel convinces the king to let them eat only the food allowed by God. This part of the story was telling people not to give up their faith.

One day the king had a dream and no one could tell him what it meant except Daniel, who had been told by God. After this Nebuchadnezzar saw that Daniel's God must be the true God. But then he changed his mind and built a giant statue and commanded that everyone worship it. Daniel's friends Shadrach, Meshach and Abednego refused and so they were thrown into a furnace. But God sent an angel to protect them and they walked out unharmed. When Nebuchadnezzar saw this, he again began to worship God.

Belshazzar, son of Nebuchadnezzar

When Nebuchadnezzar died, his son Belshazzar became king. He went back to worshipping idols. One day king Belshazzar decided to have a great feast.

During the feast a hand appeared and wrote on the wall. The king summoned Daniel who told him the writing meant that God had tested the king and found him wanting and that the days of the king were over. That night the king was killed and Darius took over the kingdom.

Darius the king

Under King Darius, Daniel was made an important person in the land and

Weblink: www.CurriculumVisions.com

he worked hard. This made others jealous. So they plotted to get rid of Daniel. They got the king to agree that for 30 days no one should be able to worship any god except Darius. They knew that Daniel would not do this, and when he refused he was thrown into a lions' den. In the den, an angel protected Daniel.

The next morning the king sent for news of Daniel and they found him unharmed. This convinced the king that they should worship the one and only true God of Daniel.

The vision

Towards the end of his life, Daniel had a vision in which he saw the coming of the Messiah *(Daniel 7:13-14)*. Daniel saw the Messiah sitting on his throne:

"… there before me was one like a son of man… He was given authority, glory and sovereign power; all peoples, nations and men of every language worshipped him. His dominion is an everlasting dominion that will not pass away, and his kingdom will never be destroyed."

▼ An angel protects Daniel when he is thrown into the lions' den and keeps him safe.

Psalms

The Psalms are among the most widely known parts of the Bible in the world.

The word 'Psalms' comes from a Greek word which means 'a song accompanied by musical instruments' and the Psalms are songs, or chants, which were accompanied by music and sung during worship in The Temple in Jerusalem. The Psalms are still used for worship today in many ways. They are written in a type of poetry (see page 31) and are very beautiful to read.

There are 150 Psalms in the Protestant version of the Old Testament. Roman Catholic and Orthodox churches include a 151st Psalm using material that was found in ancient writings called the Dead Sea Scrolls.

Who wrote them?

The Psalms were written over a long period of time, by many people. Many of the Psalms were written by King David, and others were written by King Solomon, Moses and Jewish priests or holy men.

They were written to inspire people and to create strong feelings of joy, sorrow and love of God. Many people see them as spiritual pick-me-ups.

How are they grouped?

There are different types of Psalms. The most common Psalms are laments – a cry to God from distress, pain or sorrow.

Many of these Psalms start with the word, "Why?"

Many of the Psalms thank and praise God for something that has happened. Other Psalms praise God's majesty and virtues *(8, 19, 29, 65)*; celebrate God's universal reign *(47, 93–99)*, and give thanks for the existence of ancient Israel *(46, 48, 76, 84, 122, 126, 129, 137)*. Salvation Psalms celebrate God's saving actions on behalf of His people *(66, 75)*.

Some Psalms are in praise of a king *(2, 18, 20, 45, 72, 89, 110)*. These were used during public ceremonies in ancient Israel.

How the Psalms are used today

The Psalms are also used today during Jewish and Christian worship. They are read, chanted or sung out loud.

Many of the hymns sung during Christian worship are written from the Psalms. To help with worship, the Book of Psalms is often bound

Weblink: www.CurriculumVisions.com

with the New Testament in editions of the Bible.

The New Testament uses 116 quotes from the Psalms. Psalms are a regular part of many Christian services, with most Psalms being read out in church during a year.

Why are Psalms so popular?

Psalms are among the best known parts of the Bible. In part this is because they contain verses that are beautifully written and easy to remember. Here are some examples.

Many Psalms have been used to make hymns. For example, *A Mighty Fortress is Our God* is based on Psalm 46.

"Have mercy on me O God" (Psalm 51) is also called the miserere and is the most common Psalm sung in the Orthodox church. It deals with confessing of sins.

Psalm 102 was turned into a prayer:

"Bless the Lord, O my soul;
and all that is within me,
bless his holy name!"

"The mourning of the exiles in Babylon" (Psalm 137) was turned into an African spiritual song and a pop song, *By the rivers of Babylon.*

Psalm 23, *"The Lord is my shepherd,"* is used commonly in funeral services.

Proverbs

The Book of Proverbs contains advice on how to live a good life.

God knows that we are all different kinds of people and that some of us hear His word better in one way than another. The people who wrote the Old Testament therefore gave different ways in which people could get to understand God. One of these ways was to give simple sentences or phrases which contained advice or wisdom that was easily understood. These sayings of wisdom are collected in the Book of Proverbs.

People once thought that the Proverbs were written by Solomon, but it is clear that they were written by many people, simply gathering together the wisdom of the ages.

The Book of Proverbs

The Book of Proverbs gives us a wide range of sayings, telling us about how we should behave in life. To make these easier to follow they are set as pieces of poetry, usually in two lines.

▼ Studying the Proverbs is a good way to learn more about how God wants us to behave.

Weblink: www.CurriculumVisions.com

So, when we read the Proverbs, we should remember that they were written in Hebrew poetry. This is different from much English rhyming poetry where the end words of pairs of lines rhyme. In Hebrew poetry the words are written in pairs of lines with the second line repeating the idea in the first.

The use of proverbs

You may already be familiar with many of the proverbs from the Book of Proverbs, without even realising it. This is because many of the sayings are still used today as simple examples of the correct way to behave.

Here are some examples of proverbs:

> When pride comes, then comes disgrace,
>   but with humility comes wisdom. (Proverbs 11:2)

> A wise son brings joy to his father,
>   but a foolish son grief to his mother. (Proverbs 10:1)

> A generous man will prosper; he
>   who refreshes others will himself be refreshed. (Proverbs 11:25)

> He who works his land will have abundant food,
>   but he who chases fantasies lacks judgement. (Proverbs 12:11)

> He who despises his neighbour sins,
>   but blessed is he who is kind to the needy. (Proverbs 14:21)

> A gentle answer turns away wrath,
>   but a harsh word stirs up anger. (Proverbs 15:1)

> Do not answer a fool according to his folly,
>   or you will be like him yourself. (Proverbs 26:4)

> He who is kind to the poor lends to the LORD,
>   and He will reward him for what he has done. (Proverbs 19:17)

> A gossip betrays a confidence,
>   but a trustworthy man keeps a secret. (Proverbs 11:13)

> Hatred stirs up dissension,
>   but love covers over all wrongs. (Proverbs 10:12)

Index

Abraham 5, 6, 18–19, 21, 23
Adam and Eve 14–15
Apocrypha 2, 11
Assyrian 24

Babylon 2, 8, 10, 11, 24, 26, 29

Cain and Abel 6, 15
Canaan 6, 8, 18, 19, 21, 22
Christian 4, 24, 28, 29
commandment 2, 6, 23, 24

Daniel 10, 26–27
Darius 26–27
David 8, 9, 24, 28
Dead Sea Scrolls 28
Deuteronomy 2, 8

Egypt 6, 20, 21, 22
Esau 19
Esther 10
Exodus 2, 6, 21, 22–23

Garden of Eden 14–15
Genesis 2, 6, 12–13, 14–15, 17, 18–19, 20
golden calf 6, 23
Goliath 9

Hebrew 2, 4, 12, 15, 31
hymn 28, 29

Isaac 5, 18–19
Isaiah 24–25
Israel 2, 6, 8, 9, 10, 19, 24, 25, 28
Israelite 2, 4, 6, 8, 18, 21, 22, 23

Jacob 5, 6, 19, 20, 21
Jericho 9
Jerusalem 8, 10, 24, 25, 28
Jesus Christ 2, 4, 24, 25
Jew/Jewish 4, 6, 8, 10, 11, 22, 24, 26, 28
Job 11
Jonah 10
Jordan River 8
Joseph 19, 20–21, 22
Joshua 8, 9
Judah 8, 24, 26
Judges 2, 8, 9

Leviticus 2, 8

manna 22
Messiah 2, 24, 26, 27
Middle East 2, 10
Moses 6, 8, 21, 22–23, 28
Mt Ararat 17
Mt Sinai 23

Nebuchadnezzar 26

New Testament 2, 4, 29
Noah 5, 6, 16–17, 18
Numbers 2, 8

Old Testament 2, 4–5 *and throughout*

Pharaoh 21, 22
plague 6, 22
Promised Land 2, 6, 8, 18, 23
prophet 2, 4, 10, 11, 24, 26
Proverbs 2, 11, 30–31
Psalms 11, 28–29
Purim 10

Queen of Sheba 9

Rachel 19
Rebecca 19
Red Sea 6, 22

Sabbath 8, 23
sacrifice 2, 15, 19
Sarah 18
Saviour 2, 25
Solomon 8, 9, 11, 28, 30

Ten Commandments 2, 6, 23
The Temple 8, 28
Torah 2, 4, 5
Tree of Knowledge 14

Curriculum Visions is a registered trademark of Atlantic Europe Publishing Company Ltd.

Atlantic Europe Publishing

Dedicated Web Site
There's more about other great Curriculum Visions packs and a wealth of supporting information available at our dedicated web site:

www.CurriculumVisions.com

First published in 2005 by
Atlantic Europe Publishing Company Ltd
Copyright © 2005
Atlantic Europe Publishing Company Ltd

Authors
Brian Knapp, BSc, PhD, and Lisa Magloff, MA

Religious Advisers
Reverend Colin Bass, BSc, MA, and Aella Gage

Art Director
Duncan McCrae, BSc

Senior Designer
Adele Humphries, BA

Acknowledgements
The publishers would like to thank the following for their help and advice: Hendon Reform Synagogue, Danescroft Ave, London; St James Church, Muswell Hill, London; Rector Father Terence Phipps of St James Church, Spanish Place, London.

Scripture throughout this book is taken from the HOLY BIBLE, NEW INTERNATIONAL VERSION®. Copyright © 1973, 1978, 1984 International Bible Society. Used by permission of Zondervan. All rights reserved.

Photographs
The Earthscape Editions photolibrary, except pages 12–13 *NASA*.

Illustrations
David Woodroffe

Designed and produced by
Earthscape Editions

Printed in China by
WKT Company Ltd

**What's in the Old Testament
– *Curriculum Visions*
A CIP record for this book is available from the British Library**

Paperback ISBN 1 86214 485 0
Hardback ISBN 1 86214 486 9

This product is manufactured from sustainable managed forests. For every tree cut down at least one more is planted.